THE DEVILS
WE DANCE WITH
The Alchemy of Transmuting Pain into Power

ALEXANDER
BRIAN BOWSER

Library of Congress Control Number: 2025911695

Paperback ISBN: 978-1-969063-28-2
Hardcover ISBN: 978-1-966283-62-1

1. Main category—Nonfiction › Self-Help › Personal Transformation
2. Other category—Nonfiction › Self-Help › Motivational
3. Other category—Nonfiction › Health, Fitness & Dieting › Counseling & Psychology › Trauma Psychology

Published by: AR PRESS
Roger L. Brooks, Publisher
roger@americanrealpublishing.com
americanrealpublishing.com

TABLE OF CONTENTS

To those hurting in silence,

You are not alone.

This work carries the fingerprints of many souls who stood beside me through the fires.

I am humbled to share these three reflections—

each one a mirror to different phases of this journey

THE PAST
BY EMILY FORD

When I first met Alex Bowser almost a decade ago, he was a man full of potential, but I could sense he was buried beneath pain. I could see the light in him, even when he couldn't. Back then, he was still figuring out how to turn his survival story into a healing path and I would see glimmers of hope come through. And now, standing on the other side of some of the deepest trenches a human can walk through, he's written a book that will meet you right in the middle of your own.

This isn't just a collection of stories. This is deep soul work.

Alex shares the kind of truth most people would never have the boldness to share publicly, let alone privately to their loved ones. But instead of hiding, he brings it all to the surface— so you, the reader, don't have to feel so alone in yours. The shame, the addiction, the betrayal, the self-sabotage…it's all here. But so is the redemption. The power. The awareness. The healing. The greater calling.

I've watched Alex transform before my eyes. I've watched him confront things most people run from, take accountability for his life, and rebuild from the inside out. And I've watched him use all of it. He used, every scar and every setback, as fuel to help others rise. It's such a beautiful transformation to witness.

If you're holding this book, I believe it found you for a reason. Maybe you're tired of pretending. Maybe you're carrying a past or beliefs that feel too heavy to name. Maybe you're ready to stop dimming your light and finally remember God said who you were are before the world told you who to be.

Let this book be your mirror. Let it challenge you. Let it soften you. And above all, let it remind you that healing is not only possible, it's your birthright.

With so much love,

Emily Ford

Entrepreneur, Personal Brand Expert, and Founder of FORDIFY

THE PRESENT
BY ORLANDO GOMEZ

This book is written by a good friend who I love and respect very much. One with whom I've had the privilege of working alongside over the past several years. Alex has shown himself to be very contemplative regarding the world around him and especially in self-reflection, so I wasn't surprised by the depth of thought in this book. However, I was surprised by his willingness to share so much of his personal experiences that will keep you turning the pages wanting to know more.

It is easy to talk about the good and positive things we experience in life, sharing the highlights to our Facebook's, TikTok's, and the rest of social media. However, behind every post, each person is dancing with their own devils but not willing to share how that is affecting them.

Alex's detailed honesty of the things he experienced, whether brought on by his own choices or by those things that were out of his control, is BOLD! The two things you should take away from *The Devils We Dance With* are that regardless of what you experience in life, that does not have to define you and you are not a victim, but a survivor.

Alex demonstrates at every turn how to learn from experiences, whether our mistakes or others. Never once did Alex see himself as a victim, but by using techniques through honest self-reflection, he was able to use negative experiences to learn and grow. This is his hope for you as you deal with the things preventing you from becoming the best version of yourself.

I have heard it said that there are three days in everyone's life that are unmistakable: The day you are born, the day you die, and the day that changes your life forever. Knowing Alex's heart, it is his hope that reading *The Devils We Dance With* will aid you on your journey to discover what your life is meant for.

As you begin to read, it may not be easy, but I am confident you will find it worth it.

Orlando Gomez

CEO of Stellar Solar Inc.

THE FUTURE
BY BRIANA HETHERINGTON

Alex,

I am truly at a loss for words. Thank you from the depths of my heart for sharing this with me—your vulnerability, your raw truth, and your profound wisdom are nothing short of remarkable. It takes immense courage to not only endure what you have but to articulate it in a way that allows others to see their own reflections within your journey.

Your story is a testament to the resilience of the human spirit, the power of transformation, and the unbreakable nature of the soul when it chooses to rise. You have faced depths that most fear, yet you have emerged with clarity, purpose, and a fire that illuminates a path for others. You are greatness, my friend.

I am in awe—not just of your journey, but of your ability to put into words the complexities of what it means to be human. The way you have embraced both darkness and light, turning pain into power, is nothing short of extraordinary. Your mantra, "Hurt people hurt people, healed people heal people," resonates deeply, and I believe your story will heal and awaken so many.

This letter alone carries so much depth, and I can only imagine the impact your book will have. I am honored that you shared this with me. Please know that I see you, I celebrate you, and I am beyond grateful for the light you bring into this world.

With immense gratitude and admiration,

Briana Hetherington

Entrepreneur, Author, Altruistic Advisory Life Coach

OPENING LETTER

Beautiful Soul,

The moment you were born, you cried your first tears as you took in your first breath of life. You were held and loved by your mother and father—a treasure cherished beyond words. Then you began to grow, taking your first steps, learning what life is. You explored creative wonders, adventuring far and wide with your imagination. Fearless and curious, you absorbed all the world had to offer.

Eventually, you went to school. Connecting and learning from others, a sort of social indoctrination began. Labels, cliques, and expectations crept their way into your mind. Creativity was stifled, and dreams began to wither. Ego set in, and your soul became vulnerable to conformity. You started to run other people's races, forsaking your own.

For many of us, this is what happened.

For me, this is exactly what happened.

As a result of race, society, and politics, I bought into beliefs never meant for me and started thinking a certain way because I was told to. Turns out, I was not alone. For those of us drifting through darkness, all hope is not lost—only a forgotten power:

Your Light

Imagine your soul as a purified white light, healed of everything that has tainted it. This is where our time together begins.

My name is Alexander Brian Bowser. I was born in the fall of 1991, in Denver, Colorado, to my single mother, Larisa. Like it does with many, childlike wonder took over. I was an explorer. A builder. An architect. A hero. And at times, a terror. I absorbed the world around me, both its light and its darkness.

I experienced my mother's unconditional love while also enduring the trauma of molestation at the age of five. By sixth grade, the pains of my life had become unbearable. Standing alone in our kitchen, I held a knife to my throat, ready to end it all. Seconds before completing the act, the thought of my mother finding her only child in a pool of blood calmed my hand.

With each passing year, we moved to a new town, enrolling me in a different school every time. By the age of twenty, I had relocated more than twenty times. I often joke that I have said goodbye to more best friends than some people make in a lifetime.

High school was wonderful. Filled with friends, sports, and video games, I finally had some stability. Falling in love with sports, I excelled in multiple athletic arenas. Won a few awards and set a couple records, which led to earning the respect and attention of some eyes at our local university, Fresno State. Two weeks before the '09 fall semester began, their track program granted me a ticket to perform at the NCAA level. Regardless of how successful my high school years had been, college would present significant challenges, resulting in both immense achievements and debilitating personal struggles. The false claim that I was the father of another man's child, alongside other childhood traumas, sent me spiraling into a dark period.

At nineteen years old, I left everything I'd started. My fraternity, the US Air Force's Officer Training program, and the NCAA all for a relationship with a young woman that ended in a complete obliteration of my personal identity. Everything I'd built for my life was gone.

During our time together, I would become a shell of the all-star athlete I once was. My social skills, thinking for myself, everything that was Alex Bowser, was drained by that relationship.

If I wasn't in class, I was working at her father's ranch. If I wasn't there, I was by her side. During the time we spent together, I saw my best friends maybe three times. Around seven months into our young romantic relationship, a voice began speaking to me in my head when I was away from her. It would creep in, slow at first, only to pick up until its screams clouded every other thought. For weeks, I would go to class, or work, and every day it would scream at me not to go back to her. At that time, I didn't understand where it was coming from. My own subconscious? My gut instinct? God? Being dependent on her family for work and shelter, I continued to go back, each time fighting the mental screams.

Eleven months in, Christmas came and this would be the first week we spent apart all year. Flying back home to visit my mother and father for the holiday, I found the screams finally subsided. The time away from her was what I needed to be able to reflect and work through what I had been experiencing. When I was with her, I gave in to everything she desired. I had left sports, the air force, my fraternity and friends all behind to live her life. I had literally abandoned everything that made Alex, Alex. I had become a shell of my former self. I wasn't *me* anymore, and that voice yelling at me? That was *me* trying to get me to snap out of it.

With these realizations, the peace I felt told me everything I needed to know about what needed to be done. It would just take a bit of courage. Upon boarding my return flight, I had only one thought on my mind.

It needs to end tonight.

The thought looped on repeat for two and a half hours. She picked me up from the airport to take me back to her parents, a place I called home but which had felt more like a mental prison during the last couple months. As I sat in her car, our eyes met.

"I… I can't do this anymore," I murmured, shaking.

That was all I was able to say before all hell broke loose.

The car ride was filled with screaming, tears, and the rawest of emotions, with me sitting in complete silence. After thirty minutes of driving, we finally arrived at her family's home.

Her mother opened the door for us. Seeing the tears in her daughter's eyes, she stared me down. "Alex, how could you?!" Her tone cut the threads of my soul.

Without a word, I passed by them to gather my belongings. At 11:00 p.m., I packed up my bags, loaded my Tacoma, said goodbyes to the family, and jumped in my truck. That's when it hit me.

I have nowhere to go.

I had nothing lined up. No place to stay. No job lined up. I had the clothes on my back, what I could fit in my truck, and the belief that I'd done the right thing. I was so focused on getting away from the pain that I hadn't given a single thought as to what my next move was. All I knew was I needed to go, and go now.

In the end, eleven months is all it took to go from having every opportunity to becoming a homeless couch bum. No more sports. No more fraternity. No job. No home. For a young man forged in the fires of structure and sports discipline my entire life, this was the first time I was free. Free to do anything. Experience whatever I wanted.

The result? A life fueled by sex, drugs, and electronic dance music. For the rest of my collegiate career, I became the guy snorting crystal meth in the bathroom as I earned my bachelor's in law enforcement. I laughed when they handed me my criminal law degree.

After I graduated, I went on to further my cataclysmic downward spiral only to find heaven at the bottom. What it consisted of were multiple near-death experiences, two drunk-driving accidents, and a prolonged drug rampage that ripped apart my mental, physical, and social health even further. Many times, I floored the gas pedal on the freeway, hoping it would end.

For some reason, it never did.

Each hardship became a lesson, each setback a stepping-stone, each pain turned to power, resulting in this book you now hold.

Writing over the course of five years, this journey moved me closer to the basic fundamental truth of life.

We are all human. Simply human.

Together, we are experiencing this game of life with rules created by the generations that came before us.

With the current state of the world, technology, and distractions, it is easy for our view of this simple fact to become a blurry mosaic of random days compiled together and call it a life.

This truth was reaffirmed through every brush with death, recalibrating my understanding of what it means to be human—and how some of us have lost sight of its meaning.

Human—a word frequently used, yet its essence teeters on the brink of being forgotten. With a deeper understanding, one could see how the noise of the world has drowned out the deep connection to our roots, to be different, to be unique, to be you—simply you.

Hurt People Hurt People.
Healed People Heal People.

This mantra became my guide, and I believe it can be yours as well. To seek light in the darkness and learn how to turn struggles into opportunities for growth.

The Devils We Dance With offers a raw and intimate exploration of my journey and the many paths I have walked to discover my truth. By providing you with tools and perspectives, my purpose is to help you navigate your path to discover your truth. It is not just another self-help guide or memoir—rather, it is a candid look at the lessons I've learned while facing life's darkest moments. A window into my soul.

Inside, you will find powerful narratives and practical tools to help you embrace your own unique journey. Take what resonates, apply it as you see fit, and discard the rest.

If this letter speaks to you, then this book was meant for you. Join me on this journey to remove the constraints that have bound you and navigate back to the path that will grant fulfillment.

If not, then I simply wish you the best this world has to offer.

With love and gratitude,

Alexander Brian Bowser

CHAPTER 1

ONLY THROUGH DEATH DO WE UNDERSTAND THE VALUE OF LIFE

***

#BreatheHuman

There I lay, gasping to catch my breath, a feverish sweat coating my bare skin. As I gazed at the star-filled sky, a chilling question echoed in my mind.

Is this it? Will this be how my story ends?

My cold, wet body lay shirtless atop a child's playground in the middle of a random neighborhood at four in the morning. This was the result of skating around, sniffing drugs every few minutes for hours on end. In my early twenties, these midnight cruises had become a favorite ritual. A solitary dance with empty streets under the pale white glare of the moon. There was something intoxicating about the silence, the freedom from distraction, the feeling of gliding between the stars that captivated me. Up until this point, I hadn't learned my limit with normal drugs. Which is undoubtedly why, this particular night, I found myself shirtless, vomiting, drenched in sweat, snot pouring from every orifice of my face. The events of my life had led to this singular moment, a result of a particularly dangerous synthetic concoction—bath salts, or "white dove," as the local smoke shops called it.

This wasn't the typical bath salts you bathe in but a rather potent blend of various narcotics. Combined in some foreign lab, once ingested, they offered an unpredictable and intense rush that was terrifyingly addictive. It hit fast, felt exhilarating, and provided an immense burst of energy—a dangerous three-in-one cocktail.

Often, I was asked what it felt like.

Confidently, I would reply, "It's a three-in-one—the speed of cocaine, the euphoria of Molly, and the energy of meth."

Looking back, that was more than a deadly combination. This was the compound of choice our group had grown quite fond of, and it wasn't until one weekend in particular that I realized just how dangerous it was.

One night in 2012, two friends and I were on a three-day bender. For over eighty hours, we'd partied, snowboarded, played video games, and immersed ourselves in music with, quite literally, zero sleep. Then, an unexpected email announced that we'd won tickets to a show in Los Angeles. Despite being exhausted, we checked our drug reserves and, satisfied with what remained, we made the spontaneous four-hour drive. I remember sprinting to take a shower, still wet as I put my shirt on and jumped into my buddy's car. We reached the venue only to discover that we did not win the tickets after all. In our drug fueled frenzy, we forgot to *claim* them. This meant, they went to someone else. Standing outside the arena, we looked at one another. It didn't take long for us to realize we had next to no money, no place to stay, and worst of all, no tickets—nothing. Desperation set in.

Then, with few options to choose from, one of my friends miraculously had funds on his card. He bought us general admission tickets, and we entered the venue. The artist in question had become a favorite of ours in the electro-house scene, and seeing Feed Me was highly anticipated. Excited, we made our way to the dance floor where we could rage our degenerate little faces off. Security stopped us, explaining that the floor was strictly VIP. The facial expressions shared among us said one thing, *What the* fuck?

"Yeah, sorry, man, you guys gotta go up to the balcony." Security pointed to the stairwell.

Staring down from the balcony, we felt the excitement and energy drain from the room. Our buzz had literally been killed. Frustration boiled over. Defeated, we marched back to the box office and explained the situation, asking if there was any way we could get the tickets we were supposed to have won. The manager shook his head and began to shut the door.

In a moment of desperation, my hand snatched the door, pulling it back open. "We drove from Fresno for this show. Please," I pleaded, my voice cracking, eyes wide open from the lines of bath salts I had consumed on the way down.

He paused, seeing the desperation, or perhaps he saw his younger self in us. "Wait here," he said. Twenty seconds later, he appeared with three VIP wristbands.

We were in, and the night unfolded like a scene from a movie. The music, the energy, the shared experiences—everything was heightened, but it wouldn't last. During a smoke break on the balcony, we encountered another group. One guy was completely wasted, a "wobbly"-type fellow. Sharing cigarettes, we offered some white dove for their friend. Responsibly, they asked what it was.

"It's a three-in-one. Hits as fast as cocaine, feels as good as Molly, and gives you the energy of meth," I replied, burning down the cigarette pinched between my lips.

Satisfied with my reply, they offered it to their friend, who instantly snapped out of his blackout state, switching from incoherent mumbling to coherent conversation. I had danced with this devil for a while, but there was something about seeing it with this gentleman that night that felt completely different. Something in my blind spot now crept into view.

Unfortunately, it would take some time for me to fully grasp the power of this unnatural chemical composition. Until then, the devil would play his tune and I would go on dancing, guiding others to do the same. Sometimes, I wonder how many I brought in and left behind. How many souls did I take there only to abandon them?

It's a haunting question that may never be answered.

Then came that night in the playground in 2012. Some people die for real. Some are reborn. Only a few experience an awakening. Laying with my feet hanging off the slide, I began dry heaving with nothing left to purge. Tears, chills, sweat pouring from every possible location. A whirlwind of cold and hot flashes revolved through my body. I had pushed it to the point where my body no longer knew how to regulate itself, a feeling I would experience multiple times after.

Then, an overwhelming sense of calm washed over me. My sweat dried up. No more crying. No more pain. Just bliss.

"That really almost happened, didn't it?"

However long I laid there pondering my second encounter with death, I know not. Time had escaped my senses, but I will never forget just how perfect the stars were that night. Clear, calm, and vibrant.

After replaying the events in my mind, I determined this was my rock bottom. Twenty years old and addicted to fucking bath salts. Sad to say, despite my self-awareness, I had always been a slow learner. I tended to keep myself in loops of destruction until I discovered what life was trying to teach me. I would go on repeating that night and other forms of them for a few more years to come. Looking back, I am not exactly sure how many extra lives of mine I spent. Fortunately, after enough beatings served cold by life, I figured some things out, and I am honored to share a small fraction of the beautiful life I have lived.

This is my story, and while I do not claim to have all the answers, nor is there rarely a story that possesses the knowledge suitable for all to use, mine is a true testament to the power of self-awareness and transformation. You might not relate to the specifics of drug addiction, homelessness, or sexual abuse, but you may relate to feeling disconnected from life, your purpose, or the human experience. This book speaks to the shared human struggle: to find meaning, navigate adversity, and set yourself on your path so you may rediscover what it means to be human.

It's about understanding *you,* your journey, and the power you hold to create a life of fulfillment and purpose unique to you.

Throughout the book, some heavy questions will be asked. These questions were unfamiliar to me at one point but would go on to serve as guiding stars for the development of my life.

- Are you living authentically for yourself?
- Do your actions align with your values?
- What is it that you wish to experience?

Allow my story and methods to help guide you to your truths.

CHAPTER 2

THE DEVIL IN THE NIGHT

***

Denver, CO—1996. I was five years old, living my best life. Our neighborhood was a close community with dozens of kids running around. One of my grandmother's neighbors had become a close family friend over the years. Her son, who was around five years older, quickly became an older brother to me. I spent many afternoons at their home just a few doors down, where she watched over me while my family was away. Together, he and I enjoyed countless hours of playing video games, hide-and-seek with the other kids in the neighborhood, and reveling in the joys of childhood in the '90s—having fun until the streetlights flickered on.

Then came a time when their family was staying with us at my grandmother's home. As an only child, I cherished having one of my closest friends, a boy who was like a brother, sleeping over every night. What could have been better? But life, in its unpredictable way, was about to throw me my first true curveball.

Late into the night one evening, I awoke to the sound of my creaking door sliding over the carpet. As I rubbed the sleep from my eyes, the dark crack grew wider, revealing an ominous void. My heart raced with confusion and fear about what was invading my safe space. To my surprise, I saw him—the friend and almost brother from my early childhood—emerging in the moonlight seeping through the window.

Relief washed over me, and I took a steadying breath, welcoming him into my room. He closed the door behind him and said he wanted to play a game where we took off our clothes and hugged. At the tender age of five, I had no understanding of anything sexual and the trust we shared led me to comply without hesitation. We embraced, and for the first time in my life, my genitals were touched by someone else. The sensation was overwhelming, unlike anything I had ever experienced. In my innocence, I had not even explored my own body, let alone considered that such a connection could exist with another person.

Once we finished putting our clothes back on, he made me promise to keep it a secret. If I didn't, he threatened to tell my parents. Confused and frightened, I solemnly vowed it would remain our secret. He left my room, and I drifted into a troubled sleep, grappling with my feelings. The next morning, as we crossed paths again, an unexpected bond formed between us, anchored in the silence of our shared secret—something no one else would ever know.

As the years passed, I forgot all about the night we made the pact. I moved on and the memory faded, until I started picking up on things other men would say or do. Eventually, I would share my experiences only to discover many other men had experienced similar things. For the first time, it dawned on me that I wasn't alone. Not even close. Many others have experienced something similar. Upon hearing how it affected them and how they lived their lives, I could see patterns begin to emerge—substance abuse, conflict avoidance, difficulty communicating emotions, shutting down in certain situations.

Were these all connected back to what happened when we were children? Are these all symptoms of a deep-seated trauma that we suppressed? Why aren't more of us talking about it?

A picture started coming into view. I began to understand and the more I shared my story over the years, the more I realized it is our traumas that bind us together. When you learn about what someone has endured, their pain becomes palpable and empathy surges forth. It becomes nearly impossible to harbor hatred for that person, but instead, a form of love emerges—even when you find yourselves worlds apart. This was essential to understanding how suppressing my traumas acted as an anchor pulling me down and driving impulsive sexual behavior later in my life.

After that night, I truly believed I was safe, that what had happened was a one-off, something that couldn't occur again.

Wrong.

CHAPTER 3

EMBRACING VULNERABILITY LEADS TO EMPOWERMENT

***

F ast-forward thirteen years to 2009. Now seventeen and grad-
uating a year early, I found myself enrolling in the ROTC Air
Force program at Fresno State. I joined because my good friend
Tiggy aspired to become a pilot, just like his father before him.
Given that we'd played football together since seventh grade and I
didn't really have a plan, I accepted his invitation to follow him. I
must admit the allure of fast planes and the chance to look sharp
in a uniform was too tempting to resist. Together, we walked in,
signed our names on the dotted line, and enlisted in the program.
Honestly, the thought of becoming an officer, complete with
medals and ribbons, appealed to my ego more than I cared to
admit.

In those first few weeks, I felt overwhelmed as I tried to navigate
the intricacies of the US Air Force. Between figuring out how to
integrate everything into my schedule, understanding ranks and
the chain of command, and ensuring I was always on time and
clean-shaven, one thing became clear—I was a mess of a cadet.
There was only one area where I excelled, the fitness tests. During
my first semester, I had eleven workouts a week split between
ROTC and Track. Didn't get much sleep, but I could run like a
"fucking gazelle," as I was told. This talent caught the attention
of an older cadet, one who was just about to graduate as a second
lieutenant.

As my squad commander, he took it upon himself to mentor me during those early months. We grew close enough to share calls, texts, and insider tips on how to navigate the program successfully. To me, he was a good guy. Never yelled or scolded me when I stumbled and often picked me up when other cadets were harsh. This built trust between us. Eventually, I left everything for that girl who obliterated my identity and, thus, began the journey down the dark road that landed me shirtless in the kids' playground, taunting death. He, on the other hand, continued on his journey and became a captain in the air force. We went our separate ways, and our communication came to a halt.

A couple of years after college, around 2016, he called me out of the blue. "Hey, I'm back in town. Let's catch up and grab a beer!"

"Yeah, for sure. Where and when?" I replied.

We agreed to meet at a popular bar across from our alma mater. After a few drinks and sharing stories about where life had taken us postcollege, he invited me back to his place for cigars and a bottle of Jameson—his go-to at the time.

As the night wore on and the shots were passed around, I could feel myself slipping past the intoxicated phase, into the blackout phase. This was familiar territory. I sensed the night was coming to an end, so I made my way over to his chair in the living room, nestled under the window, slumped down and muttered, "Night, man."

I'm not sure how long I was asleep, but I woke up feeling movement near my belt. As I opened my eyes, panic set in as I realized he was performing oral sex. In my drunken haze, I was far too incapacitated to react. Instead, I closed my eyes and thought, *I am too drunk to deal with this.*

The next morning, I woke up with vomit on my shirt and an excruciating headache—much worse than you'd expect from just a few beers and half a bottle of Jameson. Scanning the room, I realized I was alone. I made my way to the kitchen to clean myself up. While I gathered my things, I noticed he was still in his room, and out of courtesy, I decided not to disturb him. After all, I had a raging headache preventing me from remembering what happened the night before.

It wasn't until later that day that the memories began to resurface, and the realization hit me hard. I didn't know how to handle the situation. Should I call the cops? Should I confront him? A flood of scenarios raced through my mind, but one thing stood out—I needed to talk to him. I had to understand why he did it.

When we spoke on the phone, the words "What the fuck, man?" escaped my mouth, slicing through the air.

I could hear the fear in his voice as he responded, "I'm so fucking sorry, man. We were drunk, and I've always wanted you since college." He paused. "This was my chance."

How we handle such situations is undeniably subjective. My reaction was immediate. "That is not something *I* wanted, and you knew that," I declared firmly.

Little more was to be said, so we ended the conversation. Moving on, I suppressed it even further, pushing it to the recesses of my mind. No good would come from talking about it, or so I believed.

About two weeks later, I received another message from him—another apology, full of regret. I wasn't sure if it was my forgiving nature combined with my hazy recollection of the event, but I accepted his apology. Even though it happened, there was nothing to be done and I had to get back to living my life. So, then and there, I made the choice to lock it up, throw away the key, and get back to living. What I didn't anticipate was how it would affect me. By avoiding my childhood and now this incident, the suppressed feelings turned to rage, causing me to be angry all the time. That anger became the fuel for further self-annihilation. What I would learn from this is that shit is going to happen. How we react is entirely on us. It took me a while to figure out that the lack of awareness of the impacts of the trauma was the catalyst for me damaging not only my life but everyone else I came into contact with as well. I kept telling myself that it didn't matter and that it didn't affect me.

Couldn't have been more wrong. What I should have been asking myself was, *How is this affecting me?* and *What can I do to move past it?*

Incidents like this should never happen, but they do. I accepted what happened to me as a young boy and as a man. I am not grateful for the experience, but I am proud of myself for what I have allowed it to become. Accepting and surrendering to it has opened the doors for me to connect with others who share similar experiences. Unfortunately, it is clear and evident that this happens more often than is openly discussed. In doing so, I realized this connection is a crucial component of a healthy society. More than that, it empowers us to provide spaces for anyone who experiences something similar to make sense of what happened, understand it wasn't their fault, and equip them to move on. Embracing this responsibility taught me the difference between suppressing trauma versus accepting and surrendering. The surrender is the vulnerable part. This is how we find our flame. This is how I discovered my purpose—surviving, interpreting, and sharing my struggles to serve as a beacon of light for those who are hurting in silence.

Through this lens, "embracing vulnerability leads to empowerment"—if you allow it.

I have contemplated the traumas of my life for years, and through self-analysis, I've come to this conclusion:

Within the darkest recesses of our minds, humans possess an innate ability to bury traumas, thoughts, shame, and actions we've committed in our attempts to move on, live, and forget.

I believe the act of repressing ourselves ultimately breaks the trust we hold within.

I have interviewed hundreds of people and posed a simple question: "Why did you suppress what happened to you?"

The answer is almost always the same. "It was just easier."

This, my dear friend, strikes me as one of the root causes of diminishing the connection we have with ourselves.

Whether you have committed acts you're not proud of or have experienced something you're ashamed of, you must recognize that it's part of you. Denying a part of your mind, body, or spirit and attempting to shun it from existence does not mean it ceases to exist. That part remains within you, gaining power in the shadows and manifesting itself through other channels of your life.

When we practice repression or suppression, we can never be whole. It shifts us from survivor to victim, and when we are victims, we are not empowered. If, however, you see yourself as a survivor, then you have power. In the future, someone may need that power. They will need the strength you've gained from your pain to help them navigate their own struggles.

Moving forward, I urge you to not be ashamed of what you've experienced or of what you've done. I know it sucks, and you might be feeling a surge of emotions that need to be released. You may have to cry, break something, or express your feelings in some way—believe me, I've done all of that too. After you settle down, begin to search for the value and lessons hidden within your experiences.

CHAPTER 4

ABYSS TO PURPOSE

***

F lashback to 2012. The chilling reality of substance abuse hit me one night as I lay in bed, body wracked with chills and sweats and my central nervous system seemingly at war with itself, again. Another brutal aftermath of a drug binge, with fever, mind-splitting headaches, and dehydration, my body had become a battlefield for survival. The physical consequences, I had grown accustomed to, for however high I blasted off, I knew there was an equal trajectory down. But it was the emotional and psychological impact that was the most crushing, the creeping fear that this was how my life might end again. I remember vividly feeling as if my life was slipping through my fingers, leaving me with a deep sense of dread.

These comedowns were more than just physical discomfort. They represented the continued gradual erosion of my health. The culprit wasn't just the immediate effects of substance abuse. Years of substance abuse had led to malnutrition, muscle loss, and a steep decline in cognitive function. In less than two years, I'd lost nearly all the muscle mass I had gained as an athlete, plummeting thirty pounds to around 140. At six one, there was little to no meat on the bones. While I hadn't fully lost my mind, my morals had eroded year after year. This impairment led to choices I would never have made otherwise.

Do you know when the best time to break into cars is?

I do. Skating the streets just before sunrise, I found myself uncontrollably opening unlocked cars in a quiet neighborhood. Turns out, a good amount of people are trusting enough to leave their doors unlocked. I remember sitting in a four-door sedan, rummaging through someone's personal belongings. At that time, I was homeless, sleeping on my buddy's floor after the nasty breakup in late 2011. So naturally, any loose change was a big help. Opening compartments and checking the backseat for anything of value, I remember thinking, *Holy shit, is this really happening?* I could see what I was doing, but I didn't have control. Almost as if something else had stepped in while I sat in my mind, watching something else drive my body. Once the sun was up, whoever was piloting my body knew it was time to go. As I walked into my friend's front door around the block, he woke up from the couch.

"Where have *you* been?" He stared with one eye still closed.

I showed him the Beats headphones and other items I'd collected over the past couple hours. "Never let me do this again," I replied, shaking from the amount of cocaine coursing through my system.

The lack of judgment and complete disregard for the law—a stark contrast to my pursuit of a degree in law enforcement—was shocking. I didn't stop to consider the consequences of my actions until much later. This wasn't just about petty theft, it was a symbol of how far I'd fallen. My actions had serious repercussions, and eventually, life served me some heavy karma. My truck has been broken into multiple times and I've had some important belongings taken from me, just as I had done to others.

This illustrates the dangerous dichotomy between our higher calling and the self-destructive behavior that often accompanies substance abuse. We betray our true selves and endanger ourselves and those around us. We become negative forces, infecting the lives of those we love and poisoning the beautiful potential within us. This is a testament to the importance of prioritizing our physical and mental health, nurturing ourselves, and living a life of self-respect and integrity.

The consequences of my addiction extended far beyond the physical, to severely impacting my relationships and my sense of self-worth. I'd lost friends. My health had deteriorated to the point where I fainted twice from simply smoking a cigarette. I had become a poor influence on others, breeding destructive health patterns in those who spent time around me. This is a common trajectory for anyone struggling with addiction, whether it be substance abuse, compulsive behaviors, or other self-destructive patterns. We become both victim and agent of the problem, infecting those around us like a cancer. This underscores the importance of setting boundaries to protect our mental and emotional well-being.

The turning point came after celebrating my twenty-fifth birthday in 2016. Two others and I were drunk, drifting out into some random field like we were in *Fast & Furious* around 2 a.m. One second we were laughing, having a good time, and the next, we woke up in complete darkness, hanging sideways by our seat belts. I don't remember much up until that point, but I remember darkness all around me. No lights, no clue where I was or what was going on. Gravity pulled me down to the right where I could feel myself pressing down on another body. Unable to see anything, my hands reached out, feeling around, searching for a sign of familiarity.

A female voice pierced the darkness. "Alex?" The sober one in the group had come to first.

I held my head as it started coming back to me. "Shit, I think we rolled a few times," I stated.

She pulled out her phone and flicked the light on, revealing the situation we had found ourselves in. She was to my left, me in the middle, and then PJ was to my right, which meant he was on the bottom, where the broken glass was.

"PJ!" I tugged on him. "Bro, you good?"

Delirious, he finally came to. "Yeah, man," he said, eerily calm for just wrecking his truck.

We managed to crawl out of the vehicle, which now rested on its right side. We let out a huge cheer for surviving the accident. Looking around at one another, we high-fived and hugged for having dodged death again. Standing victorious atop the wreckage, the cold, bitter touch of reality began to set in. Three lucky idiots in the middle of a dark field, no cell service and zero sense of direction. Clouds thick above would eventually rain down on us. Sitting and huddling in the cold, we recalled what happened and the possibility of what could have happened, replaying over and over in our minds the car accident. Nearly dying. Destroying my friend's only vehicle. Would we be going to jail? Getting a DUI? The three of us freezing alone in the late-night hours felt like a prison sentence.

It would be about five hours before field workers would call the landowner and inform him there was an accident on his private property. Soon thereafter, police showed up to take a report of the incident. With the car flipped, massive drift marks stretching hundreds of feet across his field, and the random Corona bottles discarded all around his property, it was quite obvious we had been drinking and driving. The cop was pretty pissed when he couldn't prove that PJ or myself were the ones behind the wheel. Our female driver took ownership of the event and blew a zero-point-zero on the breathalyzer, clearing her of any charges. The funny thing was that she really was the one behind the wheel at the time of the incident. Any legal consequences we may have endured all came down to the owner of the property and if he wanted to press charges for trespassing and damages or let us slide.

We looked at the older gentleman. He rested his hand on his belt, his other hand using his hat to scratch his head as he surveyed his land.

"Look, uh, you kids have had a pretty bad night. I don't see any property damage, and between you guys not dying and wrecking your truck, I'm not going to press charges." He pointed around to the bottles. "Just pick all them bottles up, as much glass and plastic as you can. Get a tow truck, and we'll call it good."

Wow. We survived, no serious injuries, *and* got away from DUIs.

What? That didn't make any sense. How the heck does that even happen?

Sometimes, no logical explanation can be given. All I knew was that was the final wake-up call for me. The final variable in the equation that I needed to experience before I could climb out of this hellhole I had dragged around for over half a decade had finally presented itself. Essentially, the entire first half of my twenties had been lost, but finally, I was beginning to see a life path come into focus. After the accident, I decided it was time to rid myself of the "slow-learner syndrome."

My stepdad Dave and I met when I was four years old and had a pretty rocky start. Took us about twenty years, but together, we developed a beautiful relationship. My friends and I owe a lot to the man, probably more than we realize. Some years ago, I was in an argument with someone else and they said some things that I could not wrap my head around. Recognizing the opportunity to teach me a valuable lesson, he offered some life advice once imparted to him by his father:

> "You don't have to agree with everyone, but you should always listen to what they have to say."

That quote has been seared into my mind, and I thought it only ever meant to listen to people. It was about the time around the accident that my perception of its meaning shifted from people to the spiritual. Maybe, just maybe, the universe was trying to tell me something.

Looking within, I was troubled at what I had become. Years wasted. So many accidents. So much pain and anguish. I evaluated my life, and honestly, it felt like I had run out of lives to spare. With deep reflection, journaling, and dozens of hours of personal development videos, three insights emerged that were pivotal in my ascension:

1. **At some point I was going to be a husband and a father.** The current version of me would be a disservice to them, the family, and the society they would later then influence through their character. I needed to shed layers and fortify others to prepare for them.

2. **The necessity of actively pursuing progress and not perfection.** There is always a next level. Some levels are good to call home for a bit, but eventually, you will have to move. Forging myself into a man who can adapt and evolve with the times was important to me. Stoicism helped further my understanding in this area.

3. **How I was influencing others.** Up until this point, not only had I brushed death myself but others had walked that line with me. The night of the car accident, three families were spared the phone call where they learn their kids are not coming home. Some would say it's luck, but after so many, you start to believe in something else.

With those realizations, it was quite easy to interpret why I am still alive after all I had put myself through:

You have not yet fulfilled your purpose.

So, I figured out *why*, but now it became *where do I begin*. The answer started with a conscious decision to change my ways of thinking, behaviors, and priorities. Basically, I had to rewire my entire mind and the outlook I had on the world. What did that consist of at that time? Not a clue. The path in my mind's eye was still cloudy, unable to see the next step, but I knew I had to begin somewhere, and it started with the voice in my soul.

I did not know at the time, but every once in a while, I would get a feeling, a calling, to a specific place or gravitate to a specific person. Sometimes I would fall through a crack and slip into an opportunity where I could connect with people who would reach back to pull me forward in life. Soon, I was sitting in auditoriums, listening to prominent leaders sharing their life stories. Thousands of us listening to one person being vulnerable with their pain made me realize that I was not alone.

As I homed in on what their stories were, I saw that they shared stories of how life broke them, but they came out of hell clean on the other side. Relating to this, I realized there was hope. I realized that what I was going through was, in some twisted way, natural. The struggles, trials, and tribulations were designed to stoke the spark within. This required becoming aware of what life was trying to teach me while shedding the layers that no longer served me. From there, I needed to know how I could apply the teachings.

Ultimately, the only one who had control over which direction my life was going to go was me.

Thus, I began walking my path with purpose.

CHAPTER 5

THE DEVILS WE DANCE WITH

***

We all have things in our lives that hold us back. Persistent forces that, consciously or unconsciously, affect us day by day. They act as antagonists to our progressive nature as humans. Knowingly or unknowingly, we subject ourselves to negative influences, allowing them to dictate our actions and prevent us from living lives true to ourselves. What are these persistent antagonists?

The devils we dance with are the negative forces—emotions, relationships, activities, habits, and substances—that prevent us from progressing. These can include unhealthy coping mechanisms like excessive work, compulsive behaviors, or even things that seem positive on the surface, but ultimately, engaging with these devils disconnects us from our true potential, hindering our ability to achieve a more fulfilling existence. These negative forces pull us down from a life aligned with our purpose, preventing us from fully realizing our capabilities. We miss opportunities and our lives become unbalanced, preventing us from achieving a uniquely purposeful existence. This is a profound loss, hindering our personal journey, which prevents us from living the life we were meant to live. This chapter will explore how to identify these devils, challenge the hold they have over you, and devise steps to break free from their grip.

It's no secret that many people today are playing life small. We see it in men who mimic the trappings of manhood without ever truly embracing its responsibilities, in young women negatively influenced by flawed role models on social media who promote unhealthy lifestyles and relationships, and in the pervasive subpar behavior fueled by certain trends in music and social media that encourage instant gratification and superficial pursuits. We chase fleeting trends, seeking validation through social media and television, trying to fit into a mold we weren't designed for. This constant pressure to conform, coupled with the bombardment of often contradictory messages, creates a profound confusion about what it truly means to be human in the modern age. These are the hidden forces—the devils—that subtly shape our choices, hindering our growth and preventing us from achieving our full potential.

The consequences of these societal pressures often manifest as individual struggles with self-worth and self-care. These devils whisper insidious doubts, obscuring our self-perception and reducing our self-confidence. We wear masks of happiness, hiding our inner sadness and despair, teetering on the brink of self-destruction, constantly making choices fueled by self-doubt. We succumb to the devils' influence, justifying our inaction with excuses like, "I felt like it," "I don't like being uncomfortable," or "They treat me well," all thinly veiled justifications for avoiding discomfort and responsibility. These self-defeating patterns are the mundane excuses that diminish our innate power. They're the persistent what-ifs and past grievances that haunt us, making us forget that being human means making mistakes and learning from them. The devils reside in your mind, but manifest through your fears, lack of willpower, or naivety.

The rest of this book aims to provide you with a new perspective on life, revealing blind spots in your current worldview. To begin the journey of rediscovering yourself, let's examine your current relationships and the internal dialogue shaping your reality.

Consider your relationship with yourself—the person you see in the mirror.

Are you satisfied with what is reflected?

How about your relationships with your peers, friends, and family?

What about the voices within—are they nurturing or critical, peaceful or warring?

Don't overthink these questions yet. We'll delve deeper in the following chapters. Remember, regardless of your past experiences, you possess the potential to start anew—a choice entirely in your hands.

CHAPTER 6

HEALING YOURSELF
HEALS THE NATION

***

Having explored the broader societal context of the devils, let's now examine the specific ways these destructive forces manifest in our individual lives. We may engage in activities such as mindless dating with the swipe of an app. Participating in online porn sites to gather easy money but never knowing *who* is watching. Drug use and abuse is widely common. Casual sex with frequent partners, detached from deep connections and bonding. Compulsive social media "doom scrolling" to get the latest hit of dopamine. Remaining in toxic relationships, cultivating a negative pattern loop, blaming all but ourselves. All of which have similar underlying psychological and neurological triggers. While the specific manifestations may differ, the result is often the same—sedation, avoidance, and suppression, resulting in a numbing of our emotions and a diminished capacity for self-care.

That's where I was. All of my pain and childhood trauma led me to walk every one of those paths.

As I looked back, it was revealed they were all connected. Strung along like Christmas lights of chaos, blinking out of tune in complete disarray. All of these self-destructive behaviors, whether substance abuse, casual sex, or other forms of compulsive behavior, ultimately stemmed from an underlying void I possessed—a sense of incompleteness with a complete lack of self-awareness.

This void, often rooted in unresolved trauma or past failures, perpetuated the cycle of self-sabotage. Consistently letting people take advantage of me, people pleasing, dating the wrong kinds of women time and time again. Chaos became the norm, which, in turn, affected others and the cycle repeated until one of us broke the chain.

At some point, I began to look around at society and see what was really going on. If this is what I was experiencing, then others must be too, right? So, how are we all connected?

A theory formed.

Cancer begins in a cell or a group of cells. That group of cells affects more cells, and eventually, the system that the group of cells are part of starts to shut down. Without care, that system strains the host and disrupts the other systems. Eventually, the host will perish. It's not because the host woke up one day and suddenly had stage 4 cancer. It started in the smallest of details possible and then grew, spreading until the host could no longer fend off the disease.

The same can be said about society. A country is comprised of states. States are comprised of cities and towns. Cities and towns have neighborhoods. Neighborhoods have homes. Homes have families. Families have people.

If the people are sick with toxic behavioral patterns, the family is sick. The children grow up with that sickness, going on to impact the lives of others around them. With enough sick families, the neighborhoods are sick. Then, the towns and cities. Then the state. Eventually, the nation. This is how I see it. This is why I believe healing the individual is how you heal a nation. This is why it's so important for you to be self-aware of what is influencing you, how it is affecting you, and, in turn, how you are affecting those around you.

To embark on this journey, consider the following:

When was the last time you felt truly connected to your inner voice, the one that guides you?

Have you actively pursued that guidance, or have you allowed the whispers of self-doubt to distract you from your path?

For me, prioritizing this inner voice dramatically shifted my perspective and brought positive changes to my life, and I hope this same transformative change will occur for you as you proceed through this book.

Now, let's identify the devils *you* dance with.

CHAPTER 7

TUNE YOUR LIFE COMPASS

***

This energy map exercise will help you identify what's holding you back and what's propelling you forward, leading to greater empowerment, clarity, confidence, and self-trust. It's a powerful tool for personal transformation that, despite what happens in my life, I can come back to, apply it, and devise a new plan to move forward over and over again.

Over the past three years, I have used them in boardroom meetings, one-on-one coaching, and Zoom calls with hundreds of people. Every single time, light bulbs blink and gears begin to turn. Seeing your life's compass come into focus right before your eyes may have quite the impact.

Before you begin, ensure you are alone in a quiet or calm space. When you are in the middle of the exercise, I would advise you to *feel* rather than *think*.

RADIANT ARCHONS

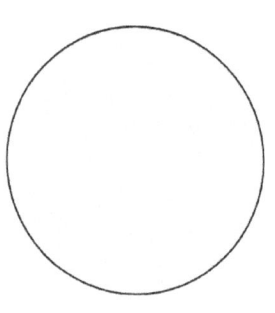

ENERGY VAMPIRES

Begin by looking at the space to the left. Understand, this is no ordinary page. Take ownership as this page belongs to you. It is your universe, with you at the center.

For those of you on the eBook version, grab a sheet of paper and draw what you see on the left.

Write your name in the middle.

Declare aloud, "I am the center of my universe."

This represents you at the center, pushing and pulling people, opportunities, and energies all around you.

Along the bottom, write Energy Vampires and underline it. From left to right, jot down the things that you *know* are draining your energy. It could be:

- Toxic relationship(s)
- Shame
- Guilt
- Bad habits
- Mental discussions you have with yourself
- Giving up
- Work
- Social media
- The news
- Family

Circle each one and draw a line connecting each vampire to your name, visualizing these as weights pulling you down.

Now, at the top under Radiant Archons, List the things that fill you with energy, joy, and purpose.

It could be a **vision**, a **dream**, a **person**, **habit**, **hobby** or **past time**. Circle each one and draw a line connecting it to your name, visualizing these as sources of energy nurturing your life.

Pause.

Look at the depicted reality you just created. What is pulling you down, and what is lifting you up?

I bet it puts things into perspective, doesn't it?

I am willing to bet those Vampires are all connected, someway or somehow, aren't they?

Now, let's set a powerful goal. Write down your biggest, most meaningful goal—something deeply personal, something you might not even have shared with others. Below it, outline three clear steps you'll take each day to move toward achieving it. Here's an example:

> Joey wanted to run a marathon, but his first achievable goal was to get his body ready to endure something of that magnitude. So, he started small. Going to the gym three times a week and adjusting his meal plan was where they started.

For me, it is what you hold now in your hands. The journey of writing this book involved confronting my own energy vampires—excessive substance use, toxic relationships, sexual rampages, and a lack of self-awareness concerning my actions and the implications they had on others' lives. It wasn't until a small trip in the back of an ambulance in Los Angeles that I encountered a spiritual awakening that transformed my life.

This exercise was a direct result of the evening when the next photo was taken. After taking more drugs than I could handle at a dubstep show, I was rushed to the hospital in the back of an ambulance. Blacking out, I felt myself drift from reality and end up in a field of loving energy. I remember thinking I had made it to heaven and how love filled my being, which was no longer physical but ethereal energy, drifting with joy. The next moment, it was black and I heard the sound of my heart monitor blipping. Opening my eyes, I could see I was handcuffed to the hospital bed with two IVs in my arms and a catheter shoved up in a rather uncomfortable location.

"Oh, you're awake. Good because your friend is here," the nurse said as my friend walked in snapping this iconic photo.

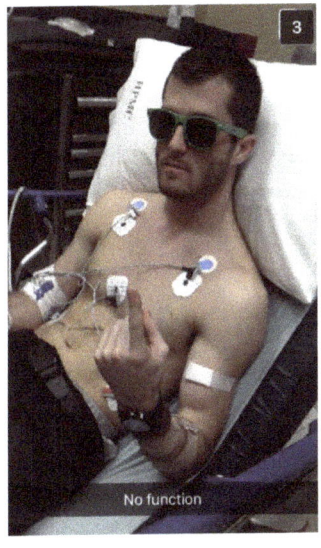

Odd to think that even in the darkest of hells, I found *my* heaven.

Over the next few weeks, I went through a mental recalibration of who I thought I was. *How did I arrive at this point in my life? How did I become that guy who gets taken away in an ambulance? What led me to this point?* In those dark moments, I found a light in the darkness, which I now share with you.

Once you have completed this exercise, examine it. Take it all in.

Do they all relate?

Do they clash?

Are you able to see where time and energy are held up?

Which one draws resources from you the most?

Typically, when working with my clients, there is a pattern that develops, and you can quite literally see the energy flowing from one affecting another.

Here is what you really need to know about them:

They exist because you are allowing them to exist.

People love beautiful lies and reject difficult truths. Do not let this be one of them.

Maybe you don't know how to say no, set personal boundaries, and fully understand what's going on, but the truth of the matter is that everything tied to those energy vampires is a result of you allowing them to have power in your life.

From here, the goal is to reduce time with, eliminate altogether, transmute negative to a positive, or simply make peace with each energy vampire.

Upon achieving this, you will naturally free up the most important currencies we have the ability to spend: time, energy, finances, and, most importantly, attention.

Where your attention goes, everything else tends to flow.

By freeing up these resources, you will naturally gravitate toward what brings you joy, purpose, and meaning, your radiant archons. When this takes place, you will effectively level up to a new reality that you have cultivated for yourself.

Tune Your Life Compass Success Stories

Joey Fettig, Colorado

He was more than a beautiful human being, and Joey and I had grown quite fond of one another in a short period of time. Encouraging each other, we made leaps and bounds with a health and well-being company, Isagenix. He won a fitness transformation contest and, sometime after that, moved to Colorado, where things began to decline. We were catching up one day, and I had mentioned to him he had been on my mind for some reason. He let me know he wasn't in a good headspace. Joey had some issues with his latest relationship, which set him on a downward spiral. Seeing where this was going, it only felt right to offer my methods and services.

"Oh shit, if the Bowser is offering, I'm definitely taking the opportunity."

We hopped on a Zoom for a couple sessions, and after completing his energy map exercise, it was easy to see that every one of his energy vampires was influenced by the one before it. Reversing the flow of dominos, we were able to see which energy vampire was the source of his spiral—weed.

As simple as it is, one energy vampire led to the decline of his daily routine. This sidetracked the time he had in the day for key habits. For a man who had always been in great spirits, fueled with an impressive drive, these two negative variables in Joey's reality played havoc with his belief system. Upon laying this out and reviewing each one, it was easy for him to see exactly what was going on and what he needed to do.

The result? Valuable resources shifted from his vampires to his radiant archons immediately. Once his habits and daily routine were back in check, his mental health shifted back into the positive. With this in alignment, he began finding joy in traveling with his dog. To this day, he's still on the path with strong boundaries set in place.

Testimonial

It's not very often you look up to someone younger than you, yet this is, without a doubt, how I perceive Alex. He is a true example of authenticity and vulnerability and has a gift of bringing to light those qualities in people blessed enough to learn from him. Oftentimes, I have felt stuck in life and didn't know how to break free. That was until Alex taught me a simple yet effective exercise to bring awareness to my energy vampires. These distractions were sucking the life out of valuable time and kept me from creating the life I desired. This single tool is something I have used countless times to eliminate what is holding me back.

—Joey

Julian Hernandez, Fresno

It's rare to meet a young man who was, in some ways, still innocent, laughing at life's jabs, and humble despite the curve balls being thrown his way. Julian is that guy.

Being a first-generation Mexican American, Julian had a simple life growing up with his family. He worked in the fields quite a bit until he caught a job with a solar installation company where he would install solar panels. Moving up through the ranks, he caught a final inspection position, which is how we met in 2020. When my solar system was installed, he inspected it.

Walking around with Julian during the inspection, I noticed how he had this infectious energy about him. We got to chatting, and he mentioned he wanted to get into sales, specifically life insurance. I knew that road and the company he was looking to sign up with. Knowing what awaited him, I invited him to our solar sales office to see if our opportunity aligned with what he was seeking. It didn't take long for him to see that what we had to offer was a much better fit.

Five years later, the young man has gone from working in the fields to inspecting solar systems to celebrating months where he would generate tens of thousands in commissions in sales. Together, we had a great time, and I love seeing his growth every step of the way.

Where did it all begin? With removing energy vampires and reinforcing resources to radiant archons.

The result? Julian has redirected his family tree for the better. The insights into life he will be able to offer as a man, husband, and father will echo down for generations to come.

Testimonial

When I first met Alex back in 2020, during the pandemic era, I had just turned twenty-one. Like many young men at that stage of life, I was searching for direction and trying to uncover my purpose. Fast-forward five years, and I'm now on a path to building the life I once only dreamed of.

Alex's mentorship has been nothing short of transformative. Through his wisdom, exercises, and unwavering belief in my potential, he opened my mind and spirit to new possibilities. With his guidance, I went from working in California's agricultural fields to contributing to the development of a multimillion-dollar sales force—a shift that seemed impossible to me at the time.

Alex didn't just teach me skills, he helped me confront my self-imposed limitations and battle the inner demons that were holding me back from reaching my true potential.

What started as a mentor-mentee relationship has grown into something deeper—I now see Alex not only as a mentor or friend but as a brother.

Thank you, Alex, for your open heart, your guidance, and your unwavering support over these years. I'm forever grateful for the impact you've had on my life.

—Julian

Katie Levine, Arizona

Katie earned her reputation as a renowned celebrity photographer in Hollywood. She has worked with many celebrities, artists, and athletes throughout her career. Her commitment to her work was of the highest caliber, and the style in which she captured her photos was nothing short of beautiful. She embodies the spirit of an artist.

I had the honor of connecting with her at a private personal branding event that our friends, Jake Havron and Emily Ford, were hosting in Santa Monica. After learning we both worked in the wedding industry, we connected deeper to what was holding our talents back from hitting the next level.

We scheduled a Zoom call and dove headfirst into her life. Able to discern the tethers anchoring her to her current state, we were able to study each of them and the nature of their power. Thirty minutes later, we picked them apart one by one, challenging their existence.

Two years later, she is absolutely crushing it. Katie has all the confidence in her abilities as a business owner, an artist, a wife, and a mother.

Testimonial

Doing the energy map with Alex helped me find clarity on what direction I should be heading and what might be holding me back. He took his time explaining all aspects to me and made me feel heard and seen while also providing insight into the elements presented.

—Katie

Jonathon Coffman, Fresno

Jonathon possesses one of those gifted minds that, once he figures something out, he takes the solution, runs up the mountain, builds an airplane, and flies back down to pick you up for a ride. I know this because this is exactly what happened.

When we met, he was a cancer survivor in his early twenties, riding a motorcycle and barely starting out his sales career. After we'd worked together from 2020–2022, he departed to open his private sales firm in the solar industry. In 2024, he purchased a home sitting on a golf course and now drives a Lamborghini with a Corvette in the garage. His journey was damn beautiful to see, but not without peril.

During the time we have known each other, he faced heartbreak, received news from the doctor that his life might be once again in jeopardy, and lost tens of thousands in commissions because of fraud. With each blow, he had every reason to give up. Each energy vampire stood ready to drain his talents before they could mature. Despite the challenges, he never took his eyes away from the vision he had for his life. Four years was all it took for him to go from broke to complete financial freedom.

He now travels the West Coast, entering his Lamborghini in car shows that allow him to connect with those who fit his future, not his past. Jonathan also moved his retired grandparents into his home and regularly takes his younger brother to theme parks. None of which was ever thought possible until he honed in on his talents, skills, and radiant archons.

His family bloodline was forever changed.

Testimonial

When I think about the impact Alex has had on my life, one phrase comes to mind: *the ultimate force multiplier.* Alex doesn't just help you see the next step—he rewires the way you view the entire staircase. His ability to pull greatness out of those around him isn't just a skill, it's his nature.

When I first met Alex, I thought I understood hard work and determination, but he showed me something deeper—the ability to take chaos and turn it into clarity, to take failure and forge it into fuel. He didn't just see potential in me—he demanded that I rise to meet it.

What makes Alex rare is that he doesn't give you answers. Instead, he asks the kind of questions that stay with you, echoing in your mind until you're compelled to act. He taught me that adversity isn't the end of the road, it's just a curve in the path, and how you navigate that curve defines your trajectory.

He didn't just believe in me—he was part of a process for me to believe in myself. And for that, I am forever grateful.

To those who have the privilege of working with Alex, buckle up. You're about to experience what happens when brilliance meets relentless determination. Here's to you, Alex, and the legacy you continue to create.

—Jonathon

CHAPTER 8

THE COMPANY YOU KEEP

***

As Jim Rohn wisely stated, "You are the average of the five people you spend the most time with." This means that the people closest to us significantly shape our thoughts, beliefs, and actions, influencing our energy.

Let's clarify what energy refers to in this context. It encompasses our emotional state, mental clarity, and overall well-being. In most cases, every relationship or human interaction, from meeting up with friends to buying groceries at the store with strangers, results in one of three outcomes.

1. A positive interaction.
2. A neutral interaction.
3. A negative interaction.

In each occurrence, relationships are either enhanced, plateau, or decline. The same could be said for substances, habits, and devices.

Positive relationships enhance our energy levels, fostering growth and self-awareness, while toxic relationships drain our energy, leading to stagnation and negativity. These relationships, found on both sides of your energy map, are some of the easiest to positively change. Strengthening radiant archons is as simple as regularly connecting and offering support without an expectation of reciprocation. Conversely, it is equally easy to minimize contact with energy vampires, but it requires awareness and willpower.

When we cultivate supportive relationships, the quality of our interactions improves dramatically. Conversations become more meaningful, perspectives are shared openly, and discussions go beyond superficial banter. By participating in these discussions, we are able to delve deeper into what it means to be human, like building stronger lives and laying the foundation for future generations. We discover alternative perspectives, broaden our worldviews, and open up to new possibilities. In essence, we become aware of perspectives previously closed off to us. From here, the lanes for stronger communities to be built on *open mindedness*, *empathy*, and *understanding* are opened—three pillars essential to a thriving society.

The company we keep either empowers us to utilize our gifts or confines us, hindering our growth and making us believe we can't achieve our potential. In some cases, those who are envious of our potential will actively work to keep us trapped.

Remember Kevin Hart's words, "People may hate you for being different and not living by society's standards, but deep down, they wish they dared to do the same."

As you grow and make positive changes, those who remain stagnant might appear to be doing worse. This is not about judgment—it's about focusing on your own journey and creating a life aligned with your personal set of values.

The people we choose to surround ourselves with profoundly impact our lives, either fueling our growth or hindering our progress. If you decide to change a variable in your life, like say, drinking, it's not just a change in behavior. To your peers, it sends a subtle yet powerful message to their subconsciouses. "If my friends are no longer engaging in self-destructive behaviors and are achieving their goals, maybe I should too." This unspoken association highlighted how my previous lifestyle had hindered my progress. By facing my energy vampires, I created space for growth. This same principle applies to any limiting relationship. The people who hold us back—the ones who discourage our aspirations and drain our energy—are the first people who we must limit access to our lives.

These energy vampires might be longtime friends, family members, or colleagues who, despite their positive qualities, drain our energy and discourage our growth. They might be those who say, "Slow down, you're making us look bad," subtly reminding us to stay within the confines of their narrow world perspective. These vampires might be a spouse, a business partner, a parent, or a coworker who actively hinders your progress and drains your motivation. I've experienced all of these.

To illustrate, consider the wolf. A wolf raised in the wild, surrounded by its pack, develops the skills and instincts to thrive. It's capable, confident, and contributes to a balanced ecosystem. However, a wolf raised in captivity, away from its natural environment, will never fully realize its potential. It might be well-cared for, but its innate strength and abilities will remain dormant. This is precisely what happens when we're surrounded by people who discourage our growth. The side effect of harnessing that power is how you affect the ecosystem of which your reality is a part. For more insight as to how an ecosystem may be impacted with or without the presence of unique powers, I recommend watching the video "How Wolves Change Rivers: Yellowstone National Park" on YouTube.[1]

You have a powerful wolf within you, and it's time to set it free. Surround yourself with a supportive pack, individuals who believe in you, who encourage your growth, and who understand the importance of nurturing your potential.

---

1   https://www.youtube.com/watch?v=fTPt70vA39k

CHAPTER 9

ACTIVITY—TAKE INVENTORY

***

This Take Inventory exercise will help you gain a clearer understanding of your relationships and how they impact your energy levels. By honestly assessing these connections, you can identify those who support your growth and those who drain your vitality. Consider your interactions over the past week.

In your journal, write down five to ten people you spend the most time with. For each person, ask yourself the following questions:

- How does this person influence me? Consider their impact on your mood, thoughts, and actions.
- How do I influence this person? Reflect on how your interactions with them affect their behavior and well-being.
- How does this person make me feel after being around them? Be honest about your emotional state after spending time with them.
- How do I make this person feel after being around them? Consider their emotional state after spending time with you.
- Is this relationship mutual, or is it singular? Does the energy flow in both directions, or does it primarily flow in one direction?
- What value is typically exchanged? What do I and this person give and receive in the relationship?
- Do I lift this person? Do I inspire and support them?

- Does this person lift me? Do they inspire and support me?
- Do I do things I don't align with when I am around certain people?
- Who do I act differently around?
- Who makes me want to be a better person?

After completing this inventory, take some time for reflection:

- Do the most important people in my life belong on the vampire side or the radiant side of my energy map?
- What am I able to do to either increase my engagement with positive relationships or reduce my contact with negative influences?
- What steps can I take to cultivate more positive relationships?
- How can I set boundaries to protect my energy from negative influences?

Be real. Be gentle. Be honest. This exercise is a powerful tool for realigning your energy.

CHAPTER 10

THE MIND IS A GARDEN: A BREATHEHUMAN SUCCESS STORY

***

In 2021, amid the lingering shadows of the COVID-19 lockdowns, I had the privilege of meeting Michael. I had previously knocked on his door to offer my solar services. He declined but not before he asked for a business card. Leaving one behind, I departed thinking nothing would come from it. About a week or two later, I was outside working in the yard, tending some weeds, when I felt the presence of someone approaching me from the side. Looking up, I saw my neighbor with whom I had left my card. Thinking he was ready to chat about solar, I welcomed him only to discover he was intoxicated and it wasn't for solar.

Hearing him out, I learned that he'd looked me up on Facebook and discovered my BreatheHuman page. Curious, he researched my methods and had an idea of what I might be able to do for him. He let me know he was highly interested in setting up a meeting to discuss what had recently taken place in his life. Sensing his pain, I agreed to it and we set a date and time to connect.

During our meeting, he shared with me that he had been looking after his mother who lost the ability to see. Day in and day out, he was with her, ensuring she had the best quality of life possible. This had been his reality for the past twenty years. Recently, she had grown ill, and after a short time, the battle with cancer led to her passing. Now alone, his daily routine, his habits, his environment had completely altered, which shook his internal belief system. This profound loss, coupled with estrangement from his father, had left Michael navigating a world vastly different from the one he had once known. During our time together, we quickly discovered something in common.

Michael and I shared a passion for gardening, an activity that we both felt transcended the simple act of planting. It served as a metaphor for life itself, where the seeds we sowed in our minds eventually blossomed into the reality we experienced. This realization became a pivotal breakthrough not only for Michael but also for me as well. The act of planting highlighted a direct correlation with the power of our thoughts, actions, and intentions.

Our lives are gardens, and we are the gardeners. Every thought, belief, and action is like a seed that can grow into either a beautiful flower or a pervasive weed. The essence of gardening—both in the soil and the soul—is the selective nurturing of the seeds that align with our deepest values and aspirations.

The mind's innate nature is to progress and evolve beyond its current state. If you plant seeds of negativity, negative experiences will expand throughout your life. Conversely, if you plant seeds of positivity and nurture them with love, empathy, and compassion, you will cultivate a life of positive experiences. For Michael, it was rediscovering himself through his passions and learning to walk a path aligned with his radiant archons.

We examined his struggles with substances like cocaine and alcohol, two dances I am extremely familiar with. Alcohol consumption erased his boundaries, which led to the next domino, cocaine. Indulging in this substance sent him on a mental spiral he would later face the consequences of in his sober state, thus creating a psychological loop he would repeat, preventing him from healing.

Fortunately, we were able to rework his relationship with alcohol, interrupting the pattern of self-sabotage. By reshaping his internal belief system, Michael was able to move past self-doubt, which gave way to an entirely new lifestyle.

The Replanting

Past missteps and dark thoughts, whether self-inflicted or implanted by others, may have once led you astray, but it's never too late to replant your garden with seeds of hope, ambition, and love. The transformation of any life from a place of despair to one filled with purpose and connection mirrors the potential for renewal and is a testament to its power.

Nurturing

For Michael, understanding that his garden, his mind, could be replanted with visions of a brighter future marked the beginning of a new chapter. By intentionally nurturing these seeds, he began to witness the blossoming of a new reality rich with opportunities, connections, and a renewed sense of purpose.

The key to treating your mind as a garden, however, is the boundaries. Knowing when to say yes and when to exercise the power of *no*.

Control Over Our Garden

The essence of our discussion is the profound control we have over the seeds we choose to nurture. What we allow to take root in our minds and hearts ultimately shapes our lives. I ask you to consider the seeds you're planting:

- What thoughts and beliefs are you nurturing?
- What needs to be "weeded" to make room for growth?
- How will you tend to your garden in the future to ensure its flourishing?

CHAPTER 11

LIFE IS AN EQUATION: RECALIBRATE YOUR REALITY

***

Belief System +Environment + Habits + Daily Routine

=

Your Reality

We are the sum total of our experiences. Those experiences—be they positive or negative—make us the person we are, at any given point in our lives. And, like a flowing river, those same experiences, and those yet to come, continue to influence and reshape the person we are, and the person we become. None of us are the same as we were yesterday, nor will be tomorrow.

—B. J. Neblet

In high school, I began to notice something elusive about life, a pattern or system that seemed to guide experiences and outcomes. It wasn't until a series of events later on that I realized life is a grand experiment—a complex formula where belief systems, environments, habits, and daily routines combine to create your unique reality.

Understanding this is crucial. Many people I've coached often fixate on the wrong variable, missing the root of their issues. Focusing on these incorrect aspects wastes time, energy, and peace of mind. Over time, this leads mainly to becoming frustrated with the process. Eventually, we give up. However, by identifying and addressing the correct variable, we can resolve problems much more quickly.

This chapter explores how to understand and manipulate these variables to transform your life from what it is now to what you envision.

It is important to understand that each new reality requires the shedding of previous variables. Some people, habits, and belief systems will sabotage your next reality. By bringing some of them with you, the probability of falling back, or "rebounding," is much greater. Consistently rebounding reduces confidence in your abilities. Reduced confidence reduces courage. No courage? No action.

No action = loop

Loop = insanity

All course correction begins with what's going on inside.

Belief Systems: The Foundation

Our belief systems form the bedrock of our existence, shaping perceptions, actions, and reactions. These are the invisible frameworks composed of values, upbringing, cultural influences, and personal experiences. Everything from our morals and principles to our attitude and religion falls within this system.

A childhood friend of mine, Mike, who served in the military, once shared an unforgettable insight. We were discussing life paths for kids from low-income areas, and he noted how many see limited career options: professional athletes, drug dealers, or rappers. This reflection made me question how our environments so powerfully shape our beliefs.

To change your reality, you must start here.

Exercise: Mapping Your Beliefs

1. **Identify limiting beliefs:** List beliefs or labels that may be holding you back. (e.g., "I'm not good enough. I belong to this group of people which means I can/cannot do this")

2. **Challenge and replace:** For each belief, assess if it truly defines you or if it's inherited from others. Replace it with empowering alternatives. (e.g., "I am capable and worthy of success. Another's belief systems are not my own")

Environment: External and Internal Influences

Your environment includes both external and internal factors that shape your reality. From the music and art you consume to the social groups you're part of and your thought patterns, these experiences shape your physical and mental state.

Environment Audit

- **People:** Consider how those around you impact your mindset. Are they supportive or draining?

- **Places:** Does your physical environment inspire or demotivate you? Evaluate your home and workplace.

- **Media:** Assess the content you consume. Is it enriching or toxic?

- **Music:** Reflect on the influence music has on you. Have you noticed your behavior change? You children's behavior? What about society?

Action Steps

Utilize newfound pain and power points in your life, and just as you did with energy vampires, think of ways to reduce time and eliminate or empower each one.

Habits: The Daily Acts of Becoming

Habits are the repetitive behaviors and thoughts that reinforce your belief system and interact with your environment. They are the building blocks of your day-to-day life.

Habit Formation Techniques

- **Habit stacking:** Pair a new habit with an existing one. For example, after brushing your teeth, meditate for five minutes.
- **Implementation intention:** Link a situation to a specific behavior. For example, think, *If I'm stressed, I take a five-minute walk.*

Choose one habit to develop that aligns with your desired reality.

Daily Routine: The Blueprint of Your Life

Your daily routine is a structured plan of your habits, executed with discipline and consistency. It directs you towards positivity, stagnation, or decline.

Designing Your Daily Routine

- **Morning ritual:** Start with something that energizes you, like exercise or meditation.
- **Learning:** Dedicate time each day to acquiring new skills or knowledge.

- **Productivity:** Schedule focused work sessions to achieve your goals.
- **Relaxation:** Include activities that rejuvenate you, physically and mentally.

Utilize the provided template to tailor your ideal day. You will need to adjust this daily as you get started.

Key Points

The Sum Total of Our Experiences

Recognizing that we are the sum of our experiences empowers us to take charge of the variables in our life equation. By consciously adjusting these variables, we can significantly alter our life's trajectory.

Transformation through Ownership

Your reality reflects the internal and external variables you've permitted to define your life. By taking ownership and committing to change, you set the stage for rapid transformation.

Conclusion: Your Life, Your Equation

Your life is an evolving equation, with each component holding the potential to drastically change your reality. By embracing this concept, you gain the freedom to experiment, learn, and ultimately create the life you've always envisioned.

Remember: the most crucial variable in your life equation is *you*.

CHAPTER 12

CHOOSE JOY

***

I once met a woman who had spent years working in a job she hated, solely focused on financial security. She felt empty and unfulfilled despite her financial success. Then, she discovered her passion for art and redirected her life. The joy and fulfillment she now experiences are a testament to the importance of aligning our lives with our passions. If we look around, it's easy to see many of us have become shells of former ourselves:

The twinkle in our eyes, faded.

The spark in our spirit, evaporated.

Void of the simple joys in life,

We become Ghosts adrift to the Winds of Strife.

A life without joy, without passion, is a tragedy with the deepest of sorrow. In this context, joy isn't fleeting happiness but a moment captured in one's life. A deep sense of fulfillment that arises from living authentically with one's values. It is not defined by societal standards or measured by external achievements like the ego.

For some, joy is found in family, impactful work, or contributing to the world. For others, it's adventure, living in the moment, or connecting deeply with others. Yet, regardless of the source, living authentically—remaining true to yourself, what you value, and being self-aware—is key. You may find this to be extremely difficult due to external circumstances. There are some elements of our lives we simply can't change, and I am not naive to this fact. Whatever you face, however, there is joy to be found in your life. For me, this involved pursuing writing and creating music, developing relationships that allowed me to experience deeper human emotions like love. I sought mentors that aligned with my values and with every step out of hell , joy was there with me. Sometimes, it is easy to find. Sometimes, it is where you decide it is.

It's cliché, but my mother always told me, "You can do anything you set your mind to," instilling a deep belief in my own abilities. From academic success to athletic achievements, each accomplishment filled me with joy throughout my life, and this belief fueled the pursuit of my ambitions. With time, I learned that achieving goals aligned with my values would bring a deep sense of fulfillment. This sense of accomplishment, however, was not without struggle, as society often pushes a narrative of negativity.

Consider the state of the world—rampant negativity often promoted by media, instilling pressure to conform to lifestyles that work for some but rarely the masses. It's easy to get swept up in this collective way of thinking. The key is to identify what brings *you* joy. Focus on that as you explore to the deepest depths you can. Allow your passions to permeate your existence. That might be as simple as the shared laughter between parent and child or glimpsing the sun's rays shine as the butterfly flutters its wings. It's about recognizing life itself is beautiful and consciously *choosing* to see the joy in the faintest of details. For me, choosing to believe everything is meant to happen as it is and surrendering to that belief served as a pillar of strength in the saddest of days.

When my grandmother, Gemma, passed away, it was one of the most depressing events to witness. To see her body shrivel away in a matter of weeks is something you're just not prepared for. The leader of our family, a woman whose strength and purity were of the highest caliber, now left a void. As a family, we could have focused on the pain and uncertainty, ready to capsize our lives, but rather, we chose to focus on the blessings she gifted us. We made peace that the time of her ascension was here. She accomplished her purpose, and it was simply time for her to go home. Focusing on the beautiful moments of her life, what she had done for the family and the elegance in which she lived her life brought us joy. That was the choice we made.

You, no matter the circumstances, will always have a choice. This is one of the greatest gifts given to us, the power to choose. Use it wisely.

CHAPTER 13

LIVING WITH GRACE

***

I t is easy to buckle under pressure, play the victim, and cast accountability aside. It's tempting to believe the world is against us and to drift through life without purpose or intention. In fact, many would argue that this has become the norm in society. Consider the lack of accountability often seen among our leaders or the frequency with which people gaslight one another. Yet, how much more do we respect those who own their mistakes and continue to move forward? What about those individuals who, despite life's relentless challenges, still greet each day with a smile and a heart full of generosity?

These individuals do exist, and my family was blessed to be led by such an exceptional soul—my grandmother, Gemma. For nearly sixty years, she was the rock of our family, embodying the power and grace that only a true matriarch can wield. Gentle and resilient, Gemma was the true measure of grace.

No matter the storm, no matter the heartache, Gemma remained calm and collected, allowing life to flow through her. She didn't suppress her experiences but accepted them as part of being human. In the spring of 2024, we lost our guiding star to an illness she couldn't overcome, and at seventy-two, our matriarch was laid to rest.

Yet, what she left behind remains eternal. As the family asked me to speak about her life, I am honored to share her story of grace with you. May it open your eyes to all there is to live for, beyond whatever pain you might be facing.

The following was the speech I gave at her life celebration:

Gemma Lee Dawson

Born August 28, 1951 –Ascended April 24, 2024

From a girl to a woman, Gemma Dawson touched countless lives. Whether stranger, friend, or family, anyone who crossed paths with Gemma experienced her love, selflessness, and genuine willingness to give the shirt off her back—a gesture many who knew her can attest to.

When tasked with writing this for the family, I was halted by a profound question. How does one summarize a life marked by such achievement and resilience, a life that stood as a mountain breaking the currents of life's hardships for her family?

During her time in this earthly realm, Gemma married my grandfather, Chip, and together they had two wonderful daughters—my mother, Larisa, and my aunt, Sandi. Their marriage, however loving, turned to divorce as Chip's struggles with alcohol overshadowed the love they once shared. As the dance with his devils took precedence over family, he was asked to leave, making my grandmother a single mother. Later, she would find love again with Larry, who became my steward grandfather. Together, they raised their children until circumstances led to his departure, leaving Gemma alone once again. Not long after, we received the heart-wrenching news of both men's premature passing, leading my grandmother to bury two loves.

Despite these trials, she never resorted to gossip or malice. I never heard her speak ill of another or complain about what she lacked. She never achieved wealth, fame, or riches, but she thanked God every day for her two daughters, who she raised with pride.

As the threads of time unwove for her, Gemma would find her true love, a man who made her laugh as they fished, our grandpa Al.

Upon examining her life, it is easy to see she lived a fulfilled life, one of adventure, love, loss, beauty, and pain. In fact, I sense she knew what it meant to be human more than most could say.

How though?

How did she bury two husbands, a son-in-law, a brother-in-law, her parents, and siblings, yet still greet each day with a smile? How did she repeatedly find love and move forward when surrender seemed easier? Over weeks of contemplation, I found the answer in one word:

Grace

At thirty-three, I've come to understand the magic of grace is a key ingredient to acceptance and fully surrendering to the ebbs and flows of life. It may be difficult to see the meaning behind what comes our way and it may not always appear perfect, but there are some things we're just not meant to understand. The beauty of it all? We don't *have* to fully understand. Sometimes, we can simply just exist to exist. But, when life does give us something we weren't ready for, we face choices. We can ask, "Why did you take her from us?" or we can embrace gratitude for all that she gave us. We are grateful she's no longer in pain, grateful for the sacrifices she made to provide her daughters a better life, grateful for the lessons learned from such a pure soul, and grateful for this moment to celebrate her life.

***

Memories of Gemma

Leading up to this moment, I had asked family members and friends to share with me their fondest memories of Gemma. To recollect on moments you shared where she impacted you for the better. Together, their collective stories shed light to her true character:

Our rock against the furious tide

A light, guiding us through the storm

An open heart that loved unconditionally

A best friend who would cause a little ruckus

Forever our family Uber driver

On a personal note, hear from those closest to her, beginning with her sister, my great-aunt Julie:

Not only was she my sister but my best friend, my confidante, my guide, my protector. Gemma taught me so much and helped me blossom into a woman. Regardless of my troubles, she was there to lend a hand, helping me through them. When my husband Steve passed, she kept me sane until Tony came into my life. Aside from our parents, Gemma loved me unconditionally. I owe her everything.

Tammy, Gemma's best friend, recalls fond memories, including a snippet from Gemma's diary when she was sixteen:

April 25, 1967—Tammy told Chip, "Drop dead and go to hell!" before hanging up on him.

A statement from her daughters, Sandi and Larisa:

Our mom was simply the best. Loved by all our friends. Many called her Mom, earning her the nickname *Gemmomma*. She volunteered much—at school functions, for Girl Scouts. She was our Uber before such a thing existed. We tried involving her in pranks, but she feared getting caught. Even so, she'd give rides to anyone in need.

Sandi recalls:

Once, she took my friend to a Michael Jackson concert because her mom wouldn't. Mom, you were the best, and if we had to do it all over, we'd choose you again.

The love for their mother was immense.

How does one achieve such a loved and revered status? Through deeper examination, it becomes clear that the true testament to Gemma's immeasurable strength was her response to life's challenges. When life hit hard, she did not fight back.

She accepted what was.

She accepted what is.

She moved forward, building a better future not only for herself but for everyone around her.

The remnants of her soul are evident in our lives. We feel her presence every time we love. We sense her spirit whenever we offer kindness to strangers, for that was Gemma. That's who she was. That's the piece of her she left with each of us.

Let her be remembered for the moments she helped you.

Let her be remembered for the times she loved you.

Let her be remembered for the grace with which she served her family, her daughters, her husband, and above all, how she served God.

Among her belongings, lovingly hoarded over decades, Sandi and the family found a note written long ago by Gemma. Today, we wish to share her final words—words that she lived by and embodied to the very core of her soul:

Life is short.

Break the rules,

Forgive quickly,

Kiss slowly,

Love truly,

Laugh uncontrollably,

And above all,

Never regret anything that made you smile.

With love,

Gemma "The Graceful" Dawson

CHAPTER 14

THE TIME MACHINE—A MEDITATION

***

Imagine for a moment that you continue the path you're on until you are eighty-five years old, lying in an old retirement facility. You have just been informed by your caretaker that you will die of heart failure in three days' time. There is no stopping this—your time on earth is about to expire.

The first day, you sign your will. All of your worldly possessions you have worked so hard to attain are no longer yours. All of the money accumulated, signed off. No longer do you own anything.

The second day, what's left of your family arrives and they say their goodbyes. They thank you for everything you have done for them. Tears are shed and final hugs are shared during your last moments together.

After your family leaves, you contemplate your life, dreams, and passions. You wonder what it would have been like to have gone left instead of right. You wonder what would have happened if you followed another path, one full of wonder and adventure.

You think back on all the missed opportunities you passed up. Loves lost. Friendships that fell apart. Maybe things could have been different.

On the morning of your final day, a young boy walks into the room. Without saying a word, the lad makes his way to the bed monitor, analyzing the readings before turning to you.

"Today's your day, isn't it?"

"Yes," you reply.

"Did you do it?" he questions.

"Do?" you reply in confusion. "What do you mean 'do'?"

"Through life, did you accomplish everything you set out to do?" the boy asks, now with a stern look.

You now realize the boy is seeking advice, and you oblige him.

"It's not that easy," you say with a bit of a chuckle and a cough.

"Yes," he states with a blank stare. "It is."

A bit more confused, you look around for a moment. "Who are you?"

He shakes his head, totally disregarding the question. "If you could go back in time and start over again, would you?"

You hesitate. "I…I'm sorry…?" you stutter aloud.

"If you had the chance to go back to a specific point in time, would you?" the boy questions as if time is running out.

"I…I guess I never really thought about that. Why do you ask?" Your eyes are now squinting as you try to decipher the boy's meaning.

The boy walks to the door, closes it, and turns to you. He begins to walk to around to the other side of your bed, eyes locked on yours. "I have the power to send you back in time to whichever age you desire. You won't remember anything between that moment and this one you're experiencing here. The only thing that you're allowed to bring back with you are your hopes, passions, and dreams. Once you're back, these will burn inside you more than they have at any other time in your life. You may choose to follow them, or you may let them go. The choice will be your own." The boy moves closer to the edge of the bed and raises his right hand, awaiting a shake in return. "What do you say?"

At this point, you need only ask yourself if you would took the ride in that time machine, and just maybe, you did. Maybe this is you in the past getting a second chance to reexperience the beauty of this world. When you view it from this lens, do your dreams and passions seem to shine a little brighter? Maybe this time, you will not worry about the little things you can't control but focus on the big things. The things that matter. The things that make you feel alive.

Too many people go through this journey called life without experiencing their own dreams or pursuing their passions. Many work their lives away at a job that they hate, forsaking their existence. They die a little bit every day without fully living this miracle. Each one of us is meant to grow into something beautiful.

To go through life without nurturing these passions—these gifts—is not only a waste of what we're restricting ourselves from experiencing but the rest of the world.

So, I pose the question once more:

Would you embark on the journey
back in time if given the chance?

Imagine, then, that you have. Allow this notion to transform your perspective, to guide your heart toward its true calling. Embrace it, chase it, and let it define you. For in this pursuit lies the essence of a life truly lived, brimming with possibilities previously unimagined.

This is your singular opportunity at life's time machine, a chance not just for existing but for a life rich in passion and fulfillment. My journey, reflecting on this choice, affirms its value. The decision to take the time machine, symbolic or not, shapes a life worth every moment. Whatever it may be, *go get it.*

Chase it.

Build it.

Become it.

You only get one chance at this life. There is no time machine.

In the end, for me, it was worth it.

CHAPTER 15

FOLLOW YOUR COMPASS

***

CONGRATULATIONS TO YOU FOR COMPLETING
THIS LEG OF YOUR JOURNEY.

I can only imagine what you went through, what you discovered about yourself, the new perspectives gained, and the fire that's been lit. I know it wasn't easy facing some of these harsh realities. Some of these challenges we didn't deserve or ask for, but in the end, we are all responsible for how we cope, learn, and react. This defines your character.

From the beginning of this project until its completion, I reimagined this book with dozens of versions over the course of five years. Suffered heartbreak once. Went financially negative multiple times in attempts to rebuild a million-dollar sales team, not once, not twice, or thrice, but four times. Had to take many months' long breaks between writing sessions. I lost confidence in my ability to complete this project twice. After disconnecting from reality during a road trip to Mount Shasta with the love of my life, I was able to ground myself. Untethered to my energy vampires, my soul aligned, acting as the conduit for creation. Finally, I could finish what I started all those years ago.

Nobody is immune to what life has in store for us. We are all subject to her winds and the direction in which she blows our rowboats. Oftentimes, the direction we float leads to a new devil on another level. Being properly equipped mentally, spiritually, and grounded in self-awareness makes the fight a hell of a lot easier.

You see, life never lets up, but if you can reduce the time it takes you to bounce back by learning to navigate rough seas, you will become a skilled sailor.

So, when life hits hard, *and it will*, ask yourself:

- How is this affecting me?
- How can I use this?
- What can I use this for?

I trust that you will find the answers within, and if they aren't clear immediately, they will surface in time. I promise.

Until then, the final question is:

Where do you go from here?

To support your continued growth, I am sharing resources that have helped me develop my mind, body, and spirit.

I have found the best time to explore these is in the morning when you wake up and in the evening before you sleep. This was crucial in rewriting my subconscious.

***

Key Terms and Ideologies

- *Ikigai* – Japanese, furthers understanding of one's purpose.
- Exercise: watch *Live to 100: Secrets of the Blue Zones* on Netflix. Episode 1.

- **Stoicism** – Founded by the Greeks and iconized by the Romans. Emphasizes the development of self-control and the practice of virtue to achieve happiness.
- Marcus Aurelius, Epictetus, Seneca
- Book: *Meditations* by Marcus Aurelius is a great start.
- *Wu Wei* – Chinese, a concept in Taoism that is about aligning with the natural flow of life and acting in accordance with the Tao (the way), which involves understanding when to act and when not to, doing so without force or struggle.
- **Duality** – Fear not the evil in the world, for, however loud and noisy it may be, rest assured, there is always an equal opposing force. Such is the nature of the universe.
- **Oxidative Stress** – I first learned of this when I worked with the Parkinson's community in Fresno. I attended the annual summit in 2019 and, upon seeing two-hundred-plus souls afflicted with Parkinson's, painted a picture of what life could be. As a result, I committed to learning what increases the probability of neurodegenerative diseases. Studying the balance between antioxidants and free radicals became the foundation for improving my physical health.
- **Fasting: Mental and Physical** – Healing the mind, body, and spirit. Sometimes you need to remove to realign.
- **Alchemy** – Transmuting one form of matter to another. Pain—Power. Victim—Survivor. Negative—Positive.
- **BreatheHuman: My Personal Ethos** – An understanding that before the color of your skin, the nationality you claim, the labels society casts upon you, you are *human* first. We are all human first. Be *human*.

With respect to those who have influenced me, I have gathered a list and brief description of who and what they represent. Countless hours have been spent learning, absorbing, and applying what these greats have shared throughout their lives. You'll notice that everyone listed has:

- Embraced vulnerability, which granted them authenticity;
- Overcome adversity from rock bottom to the apex of their lives;
- Discovered themselves through pain and turned it into power.

Select what resonates with you and dive in headfirst to continue your growth.

Les Brown: Your Gifts + Your Story + Overcome Adversity

First found Les on YouTube in 2016 and haven't been the same since. As a fellow DJ/MC I latched on to his teachings like a hawk. One of the greatest motivational speakers, Les Brown, inspires with his story of overcoming labels and adversity. He was deemed "mentally handicapped" as a child and transformed this belief with the encouragement of a substitute teacher. His journey from humble beginnings to greatness teaches us the power of belief and perseverance. Start with:

"It's POSSIBLE (Les Brown Greatest Hits)"—YouTube

Emily Ford: Serial Entrepreneur & Personal Brand Expert

Jake Havron: Transformational Speaker & CEO of Fordify

In 2019, Emily invited me to a business convention that radically changed my life. Sitting in the hotel room with her team was when I first declared I was going to create BreatheHuman.

With that one invitation, she was directly responsible for setting me on the path to sharing my story.

Emily herself went from humble beginnings, small-town girl to a complete powerhouse motivational speaker.

Together with her husband, Jake, they are helping women in business craft elegant, strategic personal brands-so they can rise above the noise, attract the right clients, and lead with confidence.

I cannot stress enough about how pivotal their impact has been on not only my life but thousands of others.

Explore their mission:

Website: FordifyMyBrand.com

Email:

Emily@itsEmily.com

Jake@JakeHavron.com

Dr. Myles Munroe: Your Gifts + Leadership + Spirituality

An esteemed educator rooted in spirituality and leadership, Dr. Myles Munroe offers profound insights into personal and societal transformation. Begin with this episode of his Leadership Series:

"How to Become a GREAT Leader?"

Simon Sinek: Leadership + Business Leadership + Open-Minded Perspective

Simon Sinek is a forward-thinking leader who explores the significance of asking, "Why?" His insights into leadership and business are transformative. Discover:

"Start With 'Why' – TED Talk from Simon Sinek"

David Goggins: Grit + Determination + Mindset

David Goggins, with his incredible story of transformation, exemplifies sheer willpower. From overcoming adversity to setting world records, his journey is a testament to resilience. Start with:

Joe Rogan Podcast

Can't Hurt Me, Audiobook

Jocko Willink: Leadership + Discipline + Accountability

Jocko Willink, a military veteran, delivers powerful lessons on discipline and accountability. Begin your exploration with:

"Get After It" Podcast

Aubrey Marcus: Spirituality + Manifestation + Higher Self

Known for his work in personal development and plant medicine, Aubrey Marcus challenges listeners to explore deeper truths. Begin with his book:

Own the Day by Aubrey Marcus

Tom Bilyeu: Mindset + Life + Personal Development

Tom Bilyeu's impactful podcast explores a range of topics from finance to spirituality, offering insights for personal and professional growth.

Explore his Impact Theory YouTube channel

Joe Rogan: Diverse Insights and Dialogue—Number One Podcast in the World

Joe Rogan's podcast spans a wide range of topics, providing thought-provoking discussions on various subjects. Some of my favorites include:

- "Paul Stamets"
- "Randy Carlson + Dr. Graham Hancock"

Garrett J. White: Getting Your Life in Order + Businessman + Truth Seeker + #WakeUpWarrior

In 2018, an ad from Garrett J. White and his team piqued my interest on Facebook. His Wake Up Warrior movement encompasses four core pillars: body, being, balance, and business. Through vulnerability and transparency, Garrett shares his journey, inspiring many to turn their lives around. Alongside his wife, he shares insights into marriage and business success across various platforms. I attended his Warrior Con in 2018, and that single convention paved the way for maturing into the man I had envisioned.

Resources:

YouTube – We Get Triggered, Episode 11 Warrior X Talks

"Be the Man" Podcast Interview with Smillion Mori

Mel Robbins: "The 5 Second Rule" + Habits + Routine

Mel Robbins is a prominent figure in personal development, known for the "5 Second Rule," which highlights how small habits can significantly impact our trajectory. Her authenticity shines as she explores why we sometimes act out of character due to our conditioned neural pathways.

TED Talk: How to Stop Screwing Yourself Over

Rea Earth: Subconscious Reprogramming + Meditations + Higher Self

Rea Earth stands out in guided meditations. Though the creator is unknown to me, their work has led to many of my meditative breakthroughs. These videos help clear mental clutter. Best listened to alone or with someone you trust, ideally, morning or bedtime.

https://www.youtube.com/@ReaEarth

Matthew McConaughey: Actor + Writer

This man has lived one hell of a life. Centered around love, adventure, and embracing the unknown, Matthew tells the tale in his personal narrative, *Greenlights.* How he conveys his understanding of life, the lessons learned and shares with his audience, is brilliant. 10/10 for me.

Audiobook version is a *must.*

***

There are many more influencers and resources that have impacted me, but these have provided immense value, perspective, and clarity. May their messages enrich your journey as they have mine.

Ultimately, your path is yours to discover.

Embrace it wholeheartedly.

CLOSING LETTER

Beautiful Soul,

From the bottom of my heart, thank you for sharing this space with me. I am certain this was not easy for you, but I hope you were able to learn from my story and understand that there is always a light at the end of the tunnel. You are not alone, no matter how much it may feel like it.

There is always another angle, lens of perception, or route to take to live your best life possible. Myself, and many before me, are living proof of that fact. So, take these lessons and apply what resonates and discard what does not. From there, I ask that you pay it forward to another, a stranger, a lover, a friend. Be there for yourself and others because, in the end, all we have is each other. Not everyone in this world sees this as a blessing but, rather, as filled with opportunities to take advantage of our brothers and sisters.

You are life itself, a spirit manifested in the physical world, and there is such beauty in knowing this.

Remember: it is always your choice to dance to the devil's tune.

Lastly—

I love you,

Your pain,

Your sorrow,

Your spirit.

I love you.

Thank you again for joining me for this brief moment. If this book has given you clarity, I would ask you to write a personal testimonial on your favorite online retailer. Not only am I eager to read what this book has done for you and the journey your path has now taken, but sharing your experience would greatly assist me in my mission to serve as a light in the darkness for anyone hurting in silence. Just be sure to speak your truth.

As for me, this book is yet another stepping-stone to climbing an even higher mountain. For now, I pass the torch unto you.

With all my being,

Alexander Brian Bowser

ABOUT THE AUTHOR

With over a decade of experience in leadership, sales training, and behavioral coaching, Alexander has dedicated his career to empowering individuals and organizations to achieve their highest potential. As a certified life coach in cognitive behavioral therapy, he brings a deep understanding of human behavior, motivation, and personal growth. His tenure in sales training across multiple industries has given him firsthand experience in building high-performing individuals.

He believes in the power of teamwork, servant leadership, and integrity. Every challenge is an opportunity to learn and embraces obstacles as a means to grow stronger, both personally and professionally. Stoicism guides his approach—staying grounded, leading with transparency, and investing in the growth of those around him. Whether it's strategizing a multimillion-dollar project or rolling up his sleeves to get the job done, Alexander's commitment remains the same: to inspire, to lead, and to create lasting impact.

In his personal life, Alex simply has a passion for life itself. For ten years, he performed across the West Coast as a DJ/MC for hundreds of weddings. In his spare time, he produces electronic music and sketches with charcoal to cultivate his creative side. When the opportunity arises, he can be found traveling the world in efforts to further his understanding of what it means to be human.

To purchase art from the book, please visit:

TheDevilsWeDanceWith.com

To connect with Alexander directly, email him at:

Alexander.Bowser@TheDevilsWeDanceWith.com

Author photo by Sarah Ward Photography

ACKNOWLEDGMENTS

To my boys who never gave up.

We ran the gauntlet and made it out together.

This book tells the story of all of us, and
without us, there is no book.

Mom, for getting me to believe I could
do anything I put my mind to.

Didn't always use it for good, but it pulled me
through to experience one hell of a life.

Dad, you showed me how to be a man and forge my own path.

Me and the boys appreciate everything you've done for us.

To my woman. Picked me up when I was beaten down
and gave us space to complete this journey together.

This is for our future.